Badass Broken Girls

BADASS BROKEN GIRLS

HOLLY RIORDAN

THOUGHT CATALOG Books

BROOKLYN, NY

THOUGHT
CATALOG
Books

Collective
World

For mama and dad. Thank you for encouraging me to pursue my passion instead of pushing me in a different direction. Thank you for always supporting me with my writing, even back when it was a train wreck.

CONTENTS

When You Lose The Love Of Your Life   1
When You Date Someone Toxic   2
When You Treat Her Poorly   3
When You Find Out He's Dating Someone Else   4
When Everyone Else Is Getting Married   5
When You Want An Old-Fashioned Love   6
When You Live Together   7
When You Accept Shit Treatment   8
When You Get Ghosted   9
When You Think You're In Love   10
When An Almost Relationship Ends   11
When He Says He Is Not Ready For A Relationship   12
When You Have Anxiety   13
When You Miss Your Old Friends   14
When You Find The Right Person   15
When He Only Wants You For Your Body   16
When You Have Trouble Trusting   17
When You Feel Unloved   18
When You Like Him More Than He Likes You   19
When You Are Tempted To Text Him   20
When You Hate What You See In The Mirror   21
When You're Told To Act Like A Lady   22
When You're Thinking About Having Sex   23
When You Dress Up   24
When You Dress Down   25
When You Need A Break From Boys   26
When You Have A One-Night Stand   27
When You Miss Someone You Never Dated   28
When You Want To Die   29
When He Cheats On You   30
When He Says He Misses You   31
When You're An Independent Woman In Love   32

When You're Being Pressured To Settle Down	33
When You're With The Love Of Your Life	34
When You Know What You Deserve	35
When Your Career Comes First	36
When You Get Married	37
When You Think Low Of Yourself	38
When He Tries To Control You	39
When Your Relationship Is About To End	40
When You Want Revenge	41
When You Want To Move Out	42
When You Grew Up Around Shitty Relationships	43
When Your Degree Feels Useless	44
When You Feel Triggered	45
When You Stalk Him Online	46
When You Are In A Bad Relationship With A Good Guy	47
When You Break Up With Them	48
When You Suck At Adulting	49
When He Takes Forever To Text Back	50
When You Feel Like A Fake	51
When You Pretend To Be Fine	52
When You Are Scared To Tell Him How You Feel	53
When You Suffer From Anxiety	54
When You Own A Dog	55
When You Run Into An Ex	56
When He Only Wants You For One Thing	57
When Your Friend Is Stuck In An Unhealthy Relationship	58
When You Get Jealous Easily	59
When You Give More Than You Get	60
When You Have Nothing To Do	61
When You Break Up	62
When You're Wasted	63
When He Keeps Sending Mixed Signals	64
When All You Do Is Fight	65
When You Are Accused Of Overreacting	66
When You Are Dating A Gentleman	67
When He's Cute But Kind Of An Asshole	68
When You Feel The Urge To Cheat	69
When You Hate Yourself For Liking Him	70
When You're Not In The Mood	71

When You're The Only One Putting In Effort 72
When Your Hope Is Gone 73
When You Get Engaged 74
When You Lose Your Best Friend 75
When You Have Self-Respect 76
When You're Still Searching For Love 77
When You Feel Like You Lost The Best Thing That 78
Ever Happened To You
When You Keep Getting Ghosted 79
When You Aren't Sure What You Want 80
When Your Ex Wants To Stay Friends 81
When They Call You Crazy 82
When You Are An Independent Woman 83
When You Still Live With Your Parents 84
When You Click With Someone 85
When You Complain Nonstop 86
When You Love Another Girl 87
When You're Waiting For Him To Make The First 88
Move
When You Text But Never See Each Other In Person 89
When You Have No Friends 90
When You Keep Your Walls Up 91
When You Aren't Living Together Yet 92
When You Have Big Dreams 93
When You Work A Minimum Wage Job 94
When He Likes Your Instagram Post 95
When You Feel Like You're Growing Apart From 96
Friends
When You Have Been Single For A Lifetime 97
When You Give Him A Second Chance 98
When You're On Your Period 99
When Everything Reminds You Of Them 100
When Your Family Is Toxic 101
When Even Television Disappoints You 102
When You Feel Weak 103
When You Are Sick Of Modern Dating 104
When You Hate Yourself For Losing Him 105
When You Still Want Him After He Hurt You 106
When You Need To Vent 107
When You Have Different Love Languages 108
When You Are Insecure In Your Relationship 109

When You Are Friends With Benefits   110
When You Stalk His New Girlfriend   111
When You Meet His Friends For The First Time   112
When You Are Insecure About Your Looks   113
When He Can't Choose Between You And Another   114
Girl
When He Is Dating Someone Else   115
When You're Dating With Anxiety   116
When You're Dating Someone With Depression   117
When You Hate Who You Are Around Them   118
When You're A Broken Girl   119
About the Author   121
You Might Also Like...   123

When You Lose The Love Of Your Life

You are not going to lose the love of your life by texting him twice. You are not going to lose the love of your life by letting him see you cry. You are not going to lose the love of your life by telling him how much you miss him and how you can picture a real future alongside him. If a boy leaves you because you refused to play games and chose to be authentic instead, then he was never meant to be yours in the first place. He was never the love of your life.

When You Date Someone Toxic

You don't want much. You just want to feel. You want to feel butterflies fluttering in your stomach. You want to feel blood twisting through your veins. You want to feel anything, everything. That's why you keeping getting stuck in such toxic relationships–because they make you feel alive. They give you a reason to cry, to scream, to scribble in your diary and belt out sad lyrics. They give you a chance to feel after being numb for far too long.

When You Treat Her Poorly

You push her away every time you take too long to answer a text. Every time you leave one of her messages unread. Every time you cancel another plan or break another promise. You push her away by acting like she's disposable. By treating her like a second choice. By reminding her that you lived without her once before and wouldn't cry any tears if you had to do it again.

When You Find Out He's Dating Someone Else

You feel like an idiot. Like you misread every word he said to you, every hug he offered you, every look he gave you. Those moments you used to replay in your mind before bed, the ones you swore were stepping stones to an official relationship, suddenly make your stomach twist. They make you wish that you never, never fell for him. They make you wish that you never had a heart at all.

When Everyone Else Is Getting Married

Stop tracing your finger along an imaginary timeline. Even though your childhood friends are settling down, it doesn't mean you should freak out about the fact that you're still single. You could find your forever person tomorrow or ten years down the line – and it wouldn't matter. Your clock isn't ticking close to zero, the sand in your hourglass isn't pouring itself empty. You have time to find love. You have time to find yourself. *You have time.*

When You Want An Old-Fashioned Love

You don't have to settle for modern love–for meeting online and talking dirty and exchanging nudes. For playing hard to get and lying about intentions and keeping the relationship casual. You can find an old-fashioned love instead. You can find a boy who will hold open doors for you and offer his jacket in the cold and agree to drive so you can relax in the passenger seat. You can be a strong and independent individual with a relationship for romantics. You can be a modern woman with an old-fashioned love.

When You Live Together

There are going to be days when they complain about the
makeup you left littered across the bathroom and days when
you're pissed they forgot to restock the ketchup. There are
going to be days when they want to be left alone and days
when you wish they would shut the hell up. But if they are
your true forever person, those days will be as rare as blue
moons, scattered throughout the calendar. The rest of the
time it will be TV marathons on the couch and dinners
cooked together. It will be cuddle sessions in your underwear
and sex on the kitchen counters. It will be waking up and
falling asleep beside your very best friend.

When You Accept Shit Treatment

Sometimes you like someone so much that you decide to sacrifice your own happiness in order to earn a sliver of time with them. You deal with missed calls and unanswered texts. You put up with weeks worth of being ignored and go right back to flirting with them as soon as they remember your existence again. You forget your own worth because you're placing too much importance on them.

When You Get Ghosted

It sucks that you are never going to know what you did wrong, that you are never going to get the closure you deserve. But you have all of the answers you need. No, he is not interested in dating you. No, he is not going to become your boyfriend. No, he is not good enough for you. Not even close.

When You Think You're In Love

You can tell that you're in love when you feel like the relationship is a gift and not a burden—even when things get rough. Even when you're low on cash and live in a cramped apartment without any food in the fridge or snacks in the cupboard. Even when you work opposite hours and have to lose sleep to see them for a small sliver of time. Even when loving them is hard, but you do it anyway because you'd choose a rough life with them over an easy life with anyone else.

When An Almost Relationship Ends

The end of an almost relationship can feel even more heart-breaking than the end of an official relationship—because you never got to fall asleep holding their hand, you never got to introduce them to your grandparents, you never got to hear those three little words escape their lips. You never created the future that you expected you would reach.

When He Says He Is Not Ready For A Relationship

If he tells you that he's not ready for a relationship, then he means he's not ready to stay up until three in the morning, cuddling and sipping coffee from your living room couch. He means he's not ready to get behind the wheel of your car and take a two-person road trip that leads nowhere but still feels euphoric. He means he's not ready to whisper sappy sweet compliments into your ear when he could be out with his friends instead, sleeping with other women instead, on his own instead. He means he is ready to break your heart.

When You Have Anxiety

Your anxiety is powerful enough to push the wrong people away, but the right people will hold their footing. They will squeeze your hand during panic attacks. They will search for tissues to clean up your tears. And when it's all over, when your heart rate returns to normal, they will remind you how much they love you and how your anxiety will never have enough power to change that fact.

When You Miss Your Old Friends

The worst thing in the world is when you miss someone who has changed. When all you want to do is reach out to them, to send them a text and meet up for coffee, but you know you're not going to get a response from the person trapped inside of your memories. You know that the person you used to stay up laughing alongside is long gone. And they aren't coming back.

When You Find The Right Person

Date someone who enhances your life. Someone who makes you excited to get up in the morning, excited to come home from work, excited to go out on the weekends. Someone who makes you excited about being alive.

When He Only Wants You For Your Body

You should never unzip your skirt to keep him around, to convince him to stay. You need to hold out for someone who wants you for more than the size of your chest or the flick of your tongue. Someone who compliments your heart, mind, and soul as often as he compliments your breasts, butt, and abs. Someone who admires the color of your aura as much as the color of your eyes.

When You Have Trouble Trusting

If you reach for the phone he left on the counter whenever he takes a shower, if you ask him to send you photographic evidence to prove that he is where he says he is, if you are suspicious of every other word that comes out of his mouth—then you need to say goodbye. Because without trust, your relationship will crumble into dust that will water your eyes. Without trust, your love never stands a chance.

When You Feel Unloved

Love is surrounding you. It is in the text your mom sends, asking if you made it home safe. It is in the secrets your friend whispers because she tells you everything first. It is on your dog's tongue as he licks your hand and in your cat's fur as she brushes up against you. You might not be in love. But you are loved.

When You Like Him More Than He Likes You

Refuse to settle for someone who isn't sure whether he wants to date you or keep his options open. Refuse to settle for an almost relationship. Half of his heart isn't enough. You deserve every little piece of him.

When You Are Tempted To Text Him

If he cared, then he would have texted you by now. If he cared, then you wouldn't be staring at a blank screen, willing his name to pop onto it. You would be in the middle of a conversation in person, face-to-face and nose-to-nose, your lips only inches away from the first of a thousand kisses.

When You Hate What You See In The Mirror

Back in high school, you chopped bangs to cover your fore-head and wore jeans to hide your thighs. You shied away from cameras and shook your head after compliments. But you're older now. You feel like you're supposed to be past the stage of self-consciousness. Of course, that stage doesn't have an age limit. For some people, it's never-ending. It refuses to go away until you decide to *push* it away. Until you decide that, yes, you are enough. Yes, you are filled with beauty. Yes, you are still that same girl you were back in high school—and that girl was damn gorgeous.

When You're Told To Act Like A Lady

Ladies can curse. Ladies can chug a beer. Ladies can get tattoos and wear ties and speak their motherfucking mind. A lady is no longer some 1950s wet dream woman who obeys everything her man orders her to do. A lady is someone with a brain. Someone with a mouth to speak and opinions to share. Someone who defines herself in any way she wants.

When You're Thinking About Having Sex

Don't sleep with him because you're worried he's going to get bored and abandon you. Sleep with him because you want to taste his lips and feel his flesh pressed against yours. Sleep with him because it's the only thing you can think about and touching him always feels right. Sleep with him because it's what you want to do, not what you feel like you *have* to do.

When You Dress Up

You are allowed to wear short skirts and clingy dresses with cleavage. You are allowed to dress in sexy clothing for yourself because it makes you feel more confident. But you are also allowed show skin because you like the compliments, you like the double takes, you like to soak up the attention.

Your skin belongs to you. Wear it however you want.

When You Dress Down

You are allowed to wear sneakers paired with sweatpants.
You are allowed to skip shaving and decide against putting
on makeup. You are allowed to focus more on what's inside
of you and what you want to accomplish during your day
than the way you look while doing so.

When You Need A Break From Boys

You don't have to spend your Saturday nights out at the bar, scoping for your forever person. You can grind against your friends on the dance floor and shoo away any guys that approach. You can climb onstage and croak karaoke to a song none of you can sing on pitch. Or you can just stay inside and make homemade sangrias to eat with an over-sized pizza pie. You can watch movies and play board games and trade secrets. You can choose to collectively forget about boys. You can stop wasting your weekends searching for someone new and start spending them with the people who already love you.

When You Have A One-Night Stand

It is okay to sleep with someone for the fun of it. It is okay to strip naked and slip beneath their covers, even though you have no desire to stick around until the morning. It is okay to embrace your sexuality because your body is a temple with doors that are allowed to open and close whenever you please.

When You Miss Someone You Never Dated

You miss funny things, the things that used to frustrate you about him. You miss trying to determine what he meant when he hugged you for a moment too long or offered to buy you dinner a little too late at night. You miss waiting up to see if he would send another text or if he would spend another day ignoring you. You miss trying to figure him out. You miss that feeling of lust. Of anticipation. Most of all, you miss thinking of *us* in the future tense instead of the past.

When You Want To Die

That musician didn't save your life by writing lyrics you could relate to in the shower. That boy didn't save your life by agreeing to go on a date with you. You saved your own life by choosing to listen to that inspiring song on repeat whenever you felt down. You saved your own life by cutting out the toxic people and keeping around the trustworthy ones. You saved your own life by doing whatever you could to stay strong. To get through your worst days and make it to a better one.

When He Cheats On You

You couldn't have stopped it from happening. He didn't cheat on you because of the way you look or because you had a fight or because you haven't slept with him enough. He cheated on you because that's what he is. A cheater. Someone who doesn't realize what he has when it's right in front of his face. Someone who is willing to throw a good girl away for one night of nothing.

When He Says He Misses You

If he tells you how much he misses you and says how you need to hang out soon, but never sets actual plans to make that happen, then he likes you—but not enough. If he liked you enough, he wouldn't have to miss you. He would rearrange his schedule to see you. He would hop on a train or sink behind the wheel of his car and drive for hours until he reached your doorstep. He would put in an actual effort to include you in his life. He wouldn't just say that he missed you. He would show you.

When You're An Independent Woman In Love

You are allowed to get butterflies when his name appears on your phone. You are allowed to have him pay for your dinner and pick you up in his car. You are even allowed to choose him over a night out with your friends. You are allowed to act like a little girl in puppy love—even though you're an independent woman. No, you don't *need* a man, but you are allowed to want one.

When You're Being Pressured To Settle Down

You were not born to be a mother. You were not born to be a wife. You have the freedom to choose those paths, but you aren't fated to fall down those paths.

When You're With The Love Of Your Life

The love of your life is someone you can sit on the couch with while the rain patters against the windowsills or sit in the car with while the radio fills the silence between you. Someone you feel completely comfortable with, even when no words are being said.

When You Know What You Deserve

You deserve bed sheets scattered with rose petals. You deserve fruit baskets and bouquets perched on your doorstep. You deserve white dresses and flutes of champagne and interlocked arms. You deserve to be spoiled by a boy who you will spoil right back.

When Your Career Comes First

Your forever person will push you toward success, not drag you away by the roots. He will encourage you to follow your passions, even if it means sacrificing time with you. Even if it means that he'll only see you for five minutes one day and ten minutes the next. No matter how much he misses you, he won't try to compete with your career, because he would rather help you reach your dreams than be the reason why you give them up.

When You Get Married

Don't make marriage the end goal—make happiness the end goal. Because some men twirl their rings at bars as they chat up strangers. Some men yank off those rings before they lean in for a kiss with their mistress. A ring doesn't prove anything. At least, not anything of value.

When You Think Low Of Yourself

You don't give yourself enough credit for everything you've achieved. You got out of bed today. You went to work today. You made your best friend laugh today. You made a stranger smile today. You might not have gotten out of that bed with the love of your life or went to work at your dream job, but you still got shit done. You still did something productive. You are forging your own path to success and you are sprinkling happiness behind you every step of the way.

When He Tries To Control You

You are not a bad girlfriend for wanting an occasional night out with your friends or for wearing low-cut shirts when you're in a room with other boys. You are not a bad girlfriend for having male friends or for spending extra hours at work. You are allowed to have a life outside of your relationship. Your boyfriend isn't meant to be the center of your universe, the authority on all that you do. He's meant to be a partner you discuss things with, not a boss you have to ask permission from.

When Your Relationship Is About To End

A baby will not save your relationship. Losing weight will not save your relationship. Having more sex will not save your relationship. If those are the only things you can think of to keep him happy, let him leave. And let him take his fucked up priorities with him.

When You Want Revenge

Keying his car is not going to do anything. Throwing a drink in his face is not going to do anything. Taking a swing at him is not going to do anything. The best revenge is to walk out of his life—completely. Delete his number from your phone. Tear his pictures off your wall. Block him on every social media platform you own. Let your silence be your best revenge.

When You Want To Move Out

One day, you won't have to hide away in your bedroom with the music turned up so loud your ears pound. One day, you won't have to listen through the door to see who else is around before you emerge from your safe place. One day, you are going to feel comfortable inside of your own home.

When You Grew Up Around Shitty Relationships

You are not destined to end up as a copy of the couples you grew up seeing. You don't have to settle your fights with fists through walls and slamming doors. You can make the decision to be better than them. To have civil conversations instead of screaming matches. To choose a healthy relationship over an easy relationship.

When Your Degree Feels Useless

Maybe you're stuck working part-time because you're struggling to land your dream job. Maybe you changed your mind and no longer want to work in the same field that you majored in. Maybe you feel like you wasted years of your life inside of a school that taught you nothing. No matter what your situation may be, your degree isn't useless, because it taught you patience. It brought you new friends. It tossed you into new experiences. You learned *something* in college—even if you learned it with a red cup in your hand instead of a book—so that piece of paper hanging on your wall isn't completely useless.

When You Feel Triggered

No one—not even your forever person—will understand what sets off your anxiety, even if they went through a similar trauma. They won't understand why you flinch when you hear the pop of a soda can. They won't understand why you shiver when you hear the mechanical hum of a garage door folding open. They won't understand how certain noises connect in your brain. Not unless you tell them. Not unless you let yourself be vulnerable and explain it to them.

When You Stalk Him Online

You tell yourself that it's not big deal, that you're just curious and it's normal to check up on old flames. But every time, the same thing happens. You see a photo or a post that makes your heart drop. That makes your stomach sink. That makes your mouth run dry and your eyes water. You just wanted a sign that he's struggling without you, that maybe he misses you too, but instead, you get proof that he's happier than he's ever been. You never get the closure you were searching for. You only discover your feelings for him aren't as faded as you thought.

When You Are In A Bad Relationship With A Good Guy

Even though he does all the right things, the relationship still feels wrong. You know you sound like a horrible person for wanting more when he already does so much for you, but unfortunately, the flowers he gives you and the texts he sends you aren't enough. And that is okay. You need more than a perfect-on-paper romance. You need someone who makes your heart flutter at hummingbird speed. You need someone you want to be with—not someone you feel obligated to be with because he's *such a good guy.*

When You Break Up With Them

Everyone knows it hurts like hell to hear *we need to talk*—but most people don't realize how hard those words are to say. It sucks to know you're going to cause tears and sleepless nights. It sucks to know that you're the bad guy in the situation, that you're the bitch, the heartbreaker. It sucks knowing that even though your ex is going to hate you for leaving, it's better this way. It's better to give them the truth than the false hope that you'll have a future together.

When You Suck At Adulting

You are allowed to ask a roommate for help cooking a home-made dinner and ask Siri how to get wine stains out of the carpet, even though you should really know how to do those things by now. You are allowed to call up your mother and cry your eyes out about how much you miss living at home and how you don't think you can do this alone. You are allowed to struggle in your twenties and beyond. No one has life figured out. No one is as put together as they seem. They're all Googling answers, just like you.

When He Takes Forever To Text Back

You hate yourself for glancing at your phone out of the corner of your eye, expecting to see his name. You hate yourself for getting excited every time the screen shivers with another notification because you haven't let go of the hope that he'll answer soon. Most of all, you hate how he can wait half a day to text you back, but as soon as you read his words, it only takes you half a second to answer.

When You Feel Like A Fake

There are a million sides to your personality. One that appears when you're dressed in a pencil skirt and surrounded by co-workers. One that comes out when you take five swallows of vodka from a cup of red plastic. One when you're half-asleep in your living room and one when you're strolling down a city street with the friends you've had since pre-school. None of those sides are inauthentic. They're all the *real* you. There are just different shades to reality.

When You Pretend To Be Fine

You are allowed to hide your pain behind false smiles and empty words. You are allowed to dodge conversations about how you've been doing lately and keep the details to yourself. But you are also allowed to break down. You can be a strong woman with tears running down her face. You can be a strong woman who needs a shoulder to lean against. You can be independent and vulnerable. Powerful and weak. Hard and soft.

When You Are Scared To Tell Him How You Feel

He might reject you. He might tell you that he isn't looking for a relationship right now or that he sees you as more of a sister than a lover. And if that happens, it's going to hurt. But it won't hurt more than staying up nights, trying to figure out whether his last text was flirtatious or friendly. It won't hurt more than wishing you would have inched closer to him and kissed him when you had the chance. It won't hurt more than wondering if you two would be together if you were brave enough to tell him how you truly felt.

When You Suffer From Anxiety

Anxiety taunts you about how ridiculous you look when you walk, when you talk, and when you chew. It convinces you that you're annoying your friends and that no boy would ever be stupid enough to love you. It warps your mind until you believe the worst. Until you wish that you could swap skins, trade brains—because you're no longer able to see the beautiful girl everybody else sees.

When You Own A Dog

You don't need a boy to spoon you at night when you have a puppy who will snuggle up on your lap. You don't need a good morning text when you can watch a tag wail whenever you walk into the room. You don't need a relationship when you have a dog that will love you harder than any human boy ever could.

When You Run Into An Ex

If you happen to see him, don't dodge him. Don't avoid eye contact with him. Don't raise your middle finger and take the opportunity to sprinkle him with insults. Say hello. Give him a hug. Plaster on a smile. Let him see how well you're doing without him, how his absence hasn't left you in pieces. Maybe it's all a lie, maybe you've never stopped thinking about him, but he doesn't deserve the satisfaction of knowing he's a wrinkle in your world.

When He Only Wants You For One Thing

Boys who beg for nudes during the first conversation, boys
who send unwanted pictures of their junk, boys who turn
every conversation into an excuse to sext, boys who invite
you over and bring you straight to the bedroom, boys who
make you think they want something real and then ghost
once they get laid—none of them are deserving of your time,
your heart, or your vagina. You are worth so much more
than your body, and anyone who fails to see that only
deserves one thing—a view of your pretty little ass as you
walk out the door.

When Your Friend Is Stuck In An Unhealthy Relationship

If she loves him enough, if she refuses to see how toxic he is, she will turn any situation around to fit her narrative. She will get pissed at you for pointing out his flaws. She will argue with you when you ask her to leave. She will cut you out of her life to make room for him. You can try to help her, you can pull when she pushes, but you don't hold enough power to save her. She has to do that herself.

When You Get Jealous Easily

Stop turning other women into your enemies. If a cute girl walks by in a clingy dress and your boyfriend stares at her, aim your anger at him instead of her. And if that boyfriend cheats with some poor girl who believed him about being single, get pissed at him. Not her. She owed you nothing. He promised you everything. He's the one who deserves the wrath. He's the one who caused your hurt.

When You Give More Than You Get

Stop handing over your whole heart to people who only scatter breadcrumbs. Stop pouring your guts out to people who are never there to catch the blood. Stop giving everything you have to people who are going to take and take and take until you turn to dust.

When You Have Nothing To Do

Adventures aren't an everyday thing. There are some days when you will have to stay inside and enjoy the fact that you're even able to experience boredom. That you're even able to complain about something so petty. You have to appreciate the fact that your lungs are taking in air, that your pulse is beating in rhythm, that you are a part of this chaotically beautiful world.

When You Break Up

At first, your limbs will feel like lead. You will struggle to pull yourself out of bed. You will feel like there's no reason to get up in the morning like you have nothing left to live for now that he's gone. You will stay beneath the covers until your eyes run out of tears until your tongue runs out of excuses to stay locked away. And when that day comes, you'll find the strength to force yourself out from your room. When that day comes, it won't feel so hard to live without him. It will actually feel *right*.

When You're Wasted

Your real friends are the ones who will wrap an arm around you when you're stumbling instead of taking pictures of you to laugh about later. Your real friends are the ones who will find you a drink of water instead of ordering you another shot. Your real friends are the ones who won't let you leave with that guy you just met and will get you safely inside of a shared Uber instead. Your real friends will take care of you, whether you're drunk or sober. Whether you think you need them or not.

When He Keeps Sending Mixed Signals

If he really wanted to date you, then he would never dream of keeping you waiting for a text even though he had time to update his snap story. He would never hit you up for a week straight and then drop out of your life out of nowhere. He would never send mixed signals because he would never want you to feel like shit.

When All You Do Is Fight

Relationships aren't supposed to be this hard. They aren't supposed to be filled with shattered promises and high-pitched screaming matches. They aren't supposed to be a contest to see who can hurt the other person worse.

When You Are Accused Of Overreacting

Don't let anyone tell you that you're overreacting, that you're being too emotional, that you need to calm down. Maybe they think you're getting upset over something silly, but that's only because they don't understand the cause of your anger. They don't understand that you're not mad about this *one* thing—that you are actually upset over the million little things that have added up over the months. They don't understand that you've been underreacting for so long that it was only a matter of time until you exploded.

When You Are Dating A Gentleman

A gentleman is someone who pulls out your chair at a restaurant and offers you their jacket in the cold. Someone who holds open the car door for you and walks you to your front stoop after a date. But a gentleman is more than that 1950s stereotype. It's someone who asks for your opinion before making a decision that will impact you. Someone who values your emotional intelligence as much as your body type. Someone who sees you as a whole person, not as a half that they need to fill to completion.

When He's Cute But Kind Of An Asshole

Flirt with him. Make out with him. Have rough, wild sex with him. But don't date an asshole who has no concern for you, who isn't willing to put in any effort with you. Don't date an asshole who believes he's way out of your league, who believes he's doing you a favor by answering your texts and calling you cute. You can't let his six-pack distract you from the truth. You can't date an asshole who will make your life a living hell.

When You Feel The Urge To Cheat

Break up with him before you have the chance to act on your impulses. Sit him down and tell him that the relationship just isn't working out, that you're sorry to do this to him, that you appreciate everything he's done for you. Do the hard thing. Do the right thing. Break up with him, because it's better than breaking his heart with an affair.

When You Hate Yourself For Liking Him

It is okay if you change your outfits three times before you leave the house because you want to look good for him. It is okay if you keep checking and re-checking your phone because you are waiting for his response to pop up on your screen. It is okay if you like him so much that you can't concentrate on your work or get anything productive done that day. It is okay to have strong feelings for someone, to let them invade your heart and mind.

When You're Not In The Mood

It doesn't matter if he bought you three drinks or if he drove you home or if he's already your official boyfriend. You don't owe him anything. Not a kiss. Not a hug. And certainly not sex. Intimacy isn't something that he earns after being nice to you a certain amount of times. Letting him touch you is your choice. Not his obligation.

When You're The Only One Putting In Effort

Relationships consist of two wholes. Two souls. Two separate individuals who are equally capable of paying for a meal and washing the dishes and doing the laundry. You should never be the only one trying. Effort should be coming from both sides.

When Your Hope Is Gone

Stay alive because your favorite band is going to come out with a new album and perform the songs in concert. Stay alive because your sister is going to get married in a few years and invite you to be a part of the party. Stay alive because you are going to get bear hugs from cute boys and learn to bake your favorite dessert and laugh with your best friend until your stomach cramps. Stay alive because you have something to live for, even if it's something that seems small.

When You Get Engaged

Make sure that you get married for the right reasons. Not because you want to wear a lace dress or snap pictures to make your Instagram followers jealous. Not because you want a ring that sparkles or a ceremony centered around your love. Not because you believe you're getting too old to keep calling your person your *boyfriend* and feel pressured to take the next step. Only marry him if you would do it all without the party or the applause. If he's your best friend and your biggest supporter. If he's the person you want to wake up next to for a lifetime.

When You Lose Your Best Friend

You are going to lose people. You are going to grow apart from some unintentionally because they went to far away colleges and created miles between you. You are going to have falling outs with others, where you dig wounds that you can never repair. You're not going to have the same exact group of friends you had in high school—and that's okay. It gives you room to make new friends. It gives you the chance to rediscover what kind of people you want to keep close and what kind of people only belong in your past.

When You Have Self-Respect

Self-respect means walking away from anyone who makes you feel like you aren't good enough, like you are some kind of burden, like you are inherently worthless—because you know that's not the truth. It means knowing that you have something unimaginable to offer this world and never letting anyone tell you otherwise.

When You're Still Searching For Love

You don't have to find your forever person in your twenties. You might not even find them in your thirties or forties. There isn't a cutoff date, a hard line between the time you're allowed to be single and when you should already be married. Some loves move like cheetahs and others move like snails.

When You Feel Like You Lost The Best Thing That Ever Happened To You

You tell yourself you're never going to feel this way again. That no one will ever compare to him. But the thing about broken hearts is they fuse themselves back together. One day, not too far in the future, that heart is going to beat hard for someone else. Those butterflies are going to regenerate. You will feel a love just as strong—even stronger—than the one you've left behind. It's only a matter of time.

When You Keep Getting Ghosted

Your dog is never going to ghost you. He is going to scamper over to the door the second he hears your shoes slapping against the pavement outside. He is going to snuggle up next to you in bed and listen with perked ears as you blabber about your day. He is going to love you unconditionally, even if you mess up, even if you make a mistake that replays in your mind every night before bed. Your dog is never going anywhere. Unlike all the boys in your life, he is able to commit.

When You Aren't Sure What You Want

It is okay to be confused. You don't need to know what career you want to pursue during your first year of college. You don't need to know the exact type of man you want to settle down with in your twenties. It is okay if you're clueless about what your future holds—and it is okay to want one thing now and change your mind later. You are always growing. You are always discovering new sides of yourself. It can take a lifetime to figure out what society pressures you to know by senior year of high school.

When Your Ex Wants To Stay Friends

Sometimes, the only way you're going to get over him is by going cold turkey. By erasing his texts from your phone. By deleting his accounts from your social media. By wiping his name from your contact list. Keeping your distance doesn't make you petty. It makes you human.

When They Call You Crazy

Sending the first text isn't crazy. Getting pissed when someone treats you like a second choice isn't crazy. Revealing your
emotions instead of trapping them inside of your chest isn't
crazy. It's brave AF.

When You Are An Independent Woman

You can still be an independent woman with stars in your eyes and butterflies in your stomach. You can still be an independent woman with your arms and legs wrapped around a man you adore. You can still be an independent woman, even though you've found the person that you refuse to live the rest of your life without.

When You Still Live With Your Parents

You feel like you are behind in life. Like you are a kid masquerading as an adult. But the secret is that everyone feels that way. Even your friends who are married. Even the ones with enough money to own their own house and raise their own kids. Everyone else is equally as confused as you. They just hide it better.

When You Click With Someone

There are some people you have known since birth who you *still* struggle to hold a conversation with whenever you get stuck in a room with them. And there are other people, people you meet unexpectedly, who you click with right away. People who can bring out your wild side when all anyone else ever sees is your shy side. People who feel like they belong in your life from the very first moment they enter it.

When You Complain Nonstop

You are always going to find something to complain about if you search hard enough. Even if you land your dream job, you will whine about the boss not treating you well enough or not promoting you soon enough. Even if you find your forever person, you will rant about him not cleaning the dishes thoroughly enough or not taking you out for dinner often enough. Stop looking for excuses to be angry and swap them out with reasons to be happy. Your emotions are within your control, so look on the shiny side.

When You Love Another Girl

Whenever you skim through an article about staying single until you find the man of your dreams or read a romantic poem about kissing your boyfriend's lips, replace *he* with *she* and *him* with *her*. Love is the same. The sentiment is the same. Nothing changes. Your prince is just a princess.

When You're Waiting For Him To Make The First Move

Stop staring at your phone screen, waiting for a notification to pop up with his name on it. Stop beating around the bush about the movie you want to see, hoping that he will ask you to go with him. Stop staring into his eyes and glancing down to his lips, wordlessly hinting that he should lean in for the first kiss. Text *him*. Ask *him*. Kiss *him*. If he is turned off by a confident woman chasing after what she wants, then he belongs in someone else's life. He has no place in yours.

When You Text But Never See Each Other In Person

He texts you right after you post an attractive picture on Instagram. He texts you at two in the morning when he's out drinking with his friends. He texts you every time he's bored and lonely and feels like flirting. But it doesn't matter how many times he reaches out to you over a screen, how often he claims that he misses you. All that matters is if he makes an effort to see you face-to-face. Does he invite you to dinner? Does he rearrange his schedule to see you? If not, then your relationship only exists over text, which means you don't really have a relationship at all.

When You Have No Friends

The world feels different after high school ends. You no longer have classes to introduce you to new faces every semester. You have to find friends in different ways. By going to concerts and talking to the stranger pushed up against you. By joining a gym and making small talk with the girl running on the treadmill to your right. By putting yourself out there the same way you would when looking for a relationship. Because friends are just like boyfriends, minus the kisses.

When You Keep Your Walls Up

You've been hurt before, so common sense convinces you to keep your heart locked in your ribcage. It orders you to push people away, to squash your feelings for boys before they blossom into something serious. But you are never going to live happily ever after unless you take a risk. Unless you are brave enough to release your heart into the wild, even though it might get clawed to shreds.

When You Aren't Living Together Yet

You don't have to prove your love to anyone by moving into a six-digit home together or getting married or posting perfectly posed pictures on Instagram. Your relationship is your own business. No one else needs to approve of it. No one else needs to validate it. As long as you two are happy, that's the only thing that matters.

When You Have Big Dreams

Never let anyone convince you that you aren't good enough, that you are being unrealistic, that it's too hard to break into the field you've been daydreaming about since you were a child. The rest of the world may have their doubts about your potential—but the only person who needs to believe in you is the girl you see in the mirror. Never let her lose hope. Never let feel defeated. Never let her abandon her biggest dreams.

When You Work A Minimum Wage Job

Never feel embarrassed about how you make your money.
You are working hard. You are putting in the hours. You are
doing something with your life instead of sitting on your ass
and hoping family members will fork over their cash. You
are surviving on your own—and that is never something to
be ashamed of saying.

When He Likes Your Instagram Post

If any other man on the planet liked your post, you would think nothing of it. It's just a click on a website. A tap on a screen. But if the boy you're interested in leaves a *like* on your newest picture? Then you waste your time wondering what it could mean. Does he think you're cute, too? Does he want to kiss you? Does he want to date you? You overanalyze every possibility. You drive yourself crazy with questions—because you play Sherlock Holmes to everything he does.

When You Feel Like You're Growing Apart From Friends

You are never going to meet up with your friends for dinner as much as you used to during teenage vacations. You are never going to gossip with them as much as you did when you passed each other in high school halls. In your twenties, your friends are going to distance themselves from you physically and maybe even emotionally. But that doesn't mean your friendship is over. It's just morphing into something new, into something more mature. Into a relationship where you could go months without seeing each other, but will still feel the same warmth whenever you meet again.

When You Have Been Single For A Lifetime

You might have your first kiss in your twenties, lose your virginity in your thirties, and get married in your forties. Reaching those milestones late in life has no correlation with your inner value. Being single only means you are intelligent enough—and patient enough—to wait for the kind of person that you deserve.

When You Give Him A Second Chance

Only give him a second chance if he promises to change. If he makes an effort to show you that he can right the wrongs of his past. If he works hard to prove that he will do whatever it takes to keep you this time. Only give him a second chance if he has actually earned one.

When You're On Your Period

Date a boy who picks up tampons for you (and grabs a chocolate bar to go with it) so you don't have to drive to the store while you're feeling bloated. A boy who doesn't act squeamish if he sees a little bit of blood. A boy who never complains about getting turned down for sex, because he knows that you're dealing with cramps and headaches that outweigh his blue-ball-problems. Date a boy who treats you well when you're cuddly and when you're moody. A boy who loves you the same every day of the month.

When Everything Reminds You Of Them

After they leave, there are going to be certain songs that hurt to hear. There are going to be shows you stop watching even though you enjoy them, and there are going to be dresses that you consider throwing out because they make you think of the romantic nights you spent together. But eventually, the wounds will sew themselves back together again and you'll be able to listen to that song and watch that show and wear that dress. You'll be able to remember the memory without letting it pick you apart.

When Your Family Is Toxic

You are allowed to cut toxic people out of your life—even if they're your sister or brother or cousin. Forget the unfinished phrase, "Blood is thicker than water," because it's only half of a whole. The entire phrase as it is meant to be read goes: "The blood of the covenant is thicker than the water of the womb." In other words, the bonds you create over the course of your lifetime are stronger than the genetics that bind you to a specific person. So if your father beats you into a hospital bed or your sister encourages you to vomit your stomach dry, then cut them out of your life. Snip their branch right off your family tree and never glance back to watch it fall.

When Even Television Disappoints You

It's okay to cry your eyes out when your favorite TV couple breaks up, when they cheat on each other and ruin their relationship. You're not stupid for getting so emotional over something created by writers in a studio—because that's not really what you're upset about. You're upset over the fact that, even on a screen, relationships never work out. You're upset about how everyone keeps raising your expectations, only to disappoint you. You're upset about how that perfect couple's darkest moments were the most realistic part of them—about how their happy relationship seemed like pure fantasy, but their breakup seemed to make perfect sense.

When You Feel Weak

You are not weak for crying your eyes out, even if it is over something silly, something that you're afraid to reach out to your friends about because they will accuse you of overreacting. You are brave for staying in touch with your true self. You are brave for letting your emotions spill from your eyes when most people shove them back inside.

When You Are Sick Of Modern Dating

You are under no obligation to play dating games. There is no rulebook requiring you to play hard to get, to wait three hours to answer a text message, to pretend you're busy when you're not. You can choose to go against the grain of the modern dating world. You can be honest about what you want instead of working hard to hide it.

When You Hate Yourself For Losing Him

You will live without him. You will thrive without him. It might not feel like it now, but you will end up happier than you've ever been without him.

When You Still Want Him After He Hurt You

Don't you dare lower your standards for him. Come to terms with the fact that he is never again going to slip into your bed at night and press his lips against your shoulder blades. He is never going to hug you from behind while you cook together in your new apartment. He is never going to surprise you on your front step with a bouquet of roses and an engagement ring. He is never going to be your happily ever after—and that is not something to mourn. That is something to celebrate.

When You Need To Vent

You are the fun friend, the one who everyone runs to with their problems, but that doesn't mean you have to keep your own feelings bundled inside. You can stop hiding behind sarcasm and death jokes and fake *I'm fines*. You can take your problems to your closest friends so they can return the favor. They would be happy to pay you back for everything you've done. They would be happy to hear what you have to say.

When You Have Different Love Languages

To you, love might mean red roses on your anniversary and jewelry wrapped in a bow beneath the tree. To him, love might mean holding hands at sunset and snuggling beneath the stars. The trick is to know your partner well enough to give them what they want—not what *you* want. You have to climb inside of your person's heart and personalize your romantic gestures for them. Show them how well you know their deepest desires.

When You Are Insecure In Your Relationship

When you are unable to see the beauty in yourself, you imagine ugliness all around you. You hallucinate problems when none exist. You doubt the boy who treats you right. You accuse the one who would never actually cheat. Of course, you don't have to listen to that tired cliché about loving yourself before you love anybody else—but it helps. Confidence makes any relationship run smoother.

When You Are Friends With Benefits

He is not your boyfriend and he has made that clear. So stop analyzing every sext he sends. Stop getting overexcited when he lets you hold his hand or cuddles you after sex. Even though it feels real to you, you made an agreement to keep things platonic. Either spill your blossoming feelings during a conversation or end the arrangement completely, because if you keep things casual with someone you truly care for, you are going to end up with a heartache too big to bear.

When You Stalk His New Girlfriend

Instead of flipping through her photographs and listing out all of her flaws, instead of directing all of your pent up hate at a girl you barely even know, be thankful that she is the one who has to deal with all of his bullshit from now on. Be relieved that you dodged a toxic bullet, that you are the one who is strong enough to live without a half-ass love like his.

When You Meet His Friends For The First Time

You might embarrass yourself by making a joke no one else finds funny. You might stutter when you introduce yourself or spill a beer across your lap. You might make the worst first impression of all time. But if your boyfriend loves you, his friends are going to love you. There's nothing to worry about when he is sitting by your side.

When You Are Insecure About Your Looks

Date someone you are comfortable waking up next to even though you haven't had a chance to put on your foundation and concealer yet. Someone you are comfortable undressing in front of even when it has been a few days since you've showered and shaved. Someone you feel beautiful in front of even when you are in your most natural state.

When He Can't Choose Between You And Another Girl

If he is considering dating someone else, make his choice easy by letting him have her. You deserve someone who wants you and only you. Someone whose feelings for you are so crystal clear that he would never dream of chasing after anyone else. Someone who believes that settling down with you was the easiest decision he has ever had to make.

When He Is Dating Someone Else

He might promise to leave her soon, but it is never going to
happen. He is telling you the prettiest lies to keep you in
place. And if he actually follows through on his promise, if
he abandons her for you, are you really okay with that? Do
you really want someone who cheats? Someone with such
low morals? Someone who might do the same exact thing to
you after you turn official? Other men are out there, faithful
men, and you can find them.

When You're Dating With Anxiety

Your fingers might tremble while texting him. You might have to breathe into a paper bag before you step out of your car to join him for dinner, or you might have to excuse yourself for the bathroom to splash cold water on your face. But the right person for you will accept your anxiety. More than that, they will fight to understand your anxiety. They will put in the effort to learn what you are going through and will help you through it the best that they can.

When You're Dating Someone With Depression

If you have a romantic night out with them, if you do everything within your power to make them smile, and the next morning they still refuse to get out of bed because their energy levels are low, you can't blame yourself. You can't question why they are so sad again when you had such a good time together. You can't blame them for not giving you the reaction you expected. You can't get angry. You can't get upset. Their sadness isn't about you. Their depression is something even they can't explain.

When You Hate Who You Are Around Them

When you're around him, you're possessive. Jealous. Easily angered. Hardly impressed. You hate who you are when you're together because somewhere deep down inside of yourself, you know that you're not supposed to be together. You're supposed to be with someone who motivates you to become the ultimate version of yourself. Someone who brings out your good side and chases away the wicked.

When You're A Broken Girl

You might feel broken because the boy you loved more than yourself stole a sliver of your heart. Now that he has faded into the distance, you have trust issues impossible to conquer. You feel like you are fucked up in more ways than you could possibly count. But you are not a wounded girl. You are a warrior. A winner. A strong, badass, goddess of a woman.

About the Author

Holly Riordan is a New York-based fiction author of horror and science fiction. She is also a full-time staff writer for Thought Catalog.

Twitter
@HollyyRio
Instagram
@hollyyrio
Facebook
facebook.com/hollyriordanwriting/
Website
thoughtcatalog.com/holly-riordan/

YOU MIGHT ALSO LIKE:

Lifeless Souls
by Holly Riordan

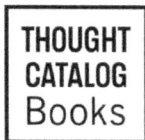

If You Were Still Alive
by Holly Riordan

Severe(d)
by Holly Riordan

THOUGHT
CATALOG
Books